My Buddy, Dido!

written by
Marion Mutala

illustrated by
Olha Tkachenko

My Buddy, Dido!
Text © Marion Mutala, 2018
Illustrations © Olha Tkachenko 2018

Second edition July 2023

Cataloguing data available from Library and Archives Canada

ISBN 978-1-7390670-2-1
ebook 978-1-7390670-3-8

Border design © www.istockphoto.com/Oksana Stuk
Author photo © Marin Hyrniuk
Illustrator photo © Bruce Blom
Creative consultant: Lori Burton
Edited by Heather Nickel and Lori Burton
Layout and design by Heather Nickel
Second edition layout and editing by Little Details Editing

With special thanks to Olha Tkachenko for her lovely illustrations,
Kate Hodgson for her beautiful word cloud, and Heather Nickel and
Lori Burton for their fine publishing insight.

Printed in Canada

Millennium Marketing
Saskatoon, SK

MILLENNIUM MARKETING

Dziadek
nonno
Opa
avus
grand-père
Taid
Grandfather
lolo
nagyapa
Opa
umushumimau
Büyük baba
ojiisan
seanathair
athair crionna
祖父
dido
avô
Παππούς
Groβvater
grandfather
avus
vanaisa
snva
avus
Nimosom
vanaisa
seanathair
Opa
edo
Nagya
deda
vectēvs
Opa ataatatsiag
할아버지
zaydeh
grand-père
deda
deda
abuelo
farfar
jaddi
sabba
kuku kane
Dido
mosom
senelis
senelis
avus
nimisom
Taid
mosom
kuku kane
Raksótha ki:ken
Raksótha ki:ken
umushumimau

Author's Note

In 1891, Ukrainians first immigrated to Canada from what is now Ukraine. This book is dedicated not only to those Ukrainian pioneers, but to men from all cultures, especially those who chose to make their homes on the Canadian Prairies—men such as my late dido, Stefan Dubyk, who came to Canada in 1911, and my late dad, August Mutala, who emigrated from Slovakia in 1930.

Giant, short, plump or small.
Thin-haired, long-haired, toupée-haired, bald.
Every colour, build and size.
Cheerful, silly, fun-loving, wise.

My buddy, Dido!

Don't need more sugar, though I do like to eat.
What I want is Dido's big feet
to dance me around with his hugs so sweet.

My buddy, Dido!

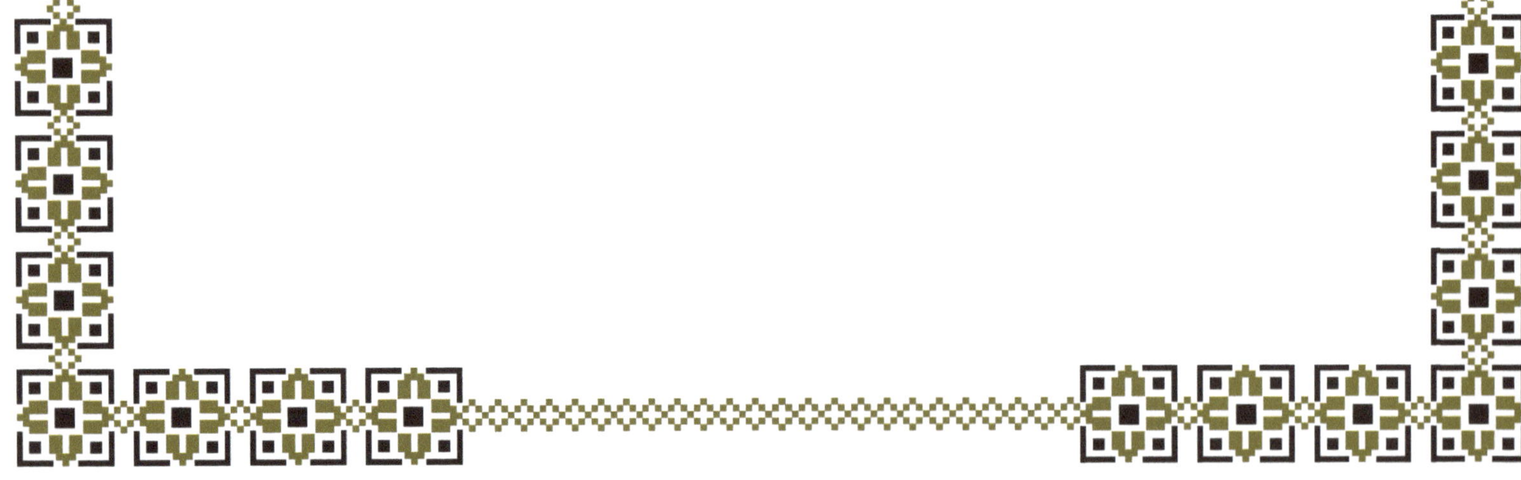

Don't need more money, though I like to buy stuff.
What I want (whether goofy or gruff)
is Dido's smile—it's enough.

My buddy, Dido!

КОБЗАР

Don't need more playthings, not a one.
I want my dido when the day is done
to read me a story in Ukrai-ni-an.

My buddy, Dido!

Don't need ice cream, though I like two scoops.
When I need energy for shooting hoops,
I want Dido's bread with *holushki* soup.

My buddy, Dido!

MAPS

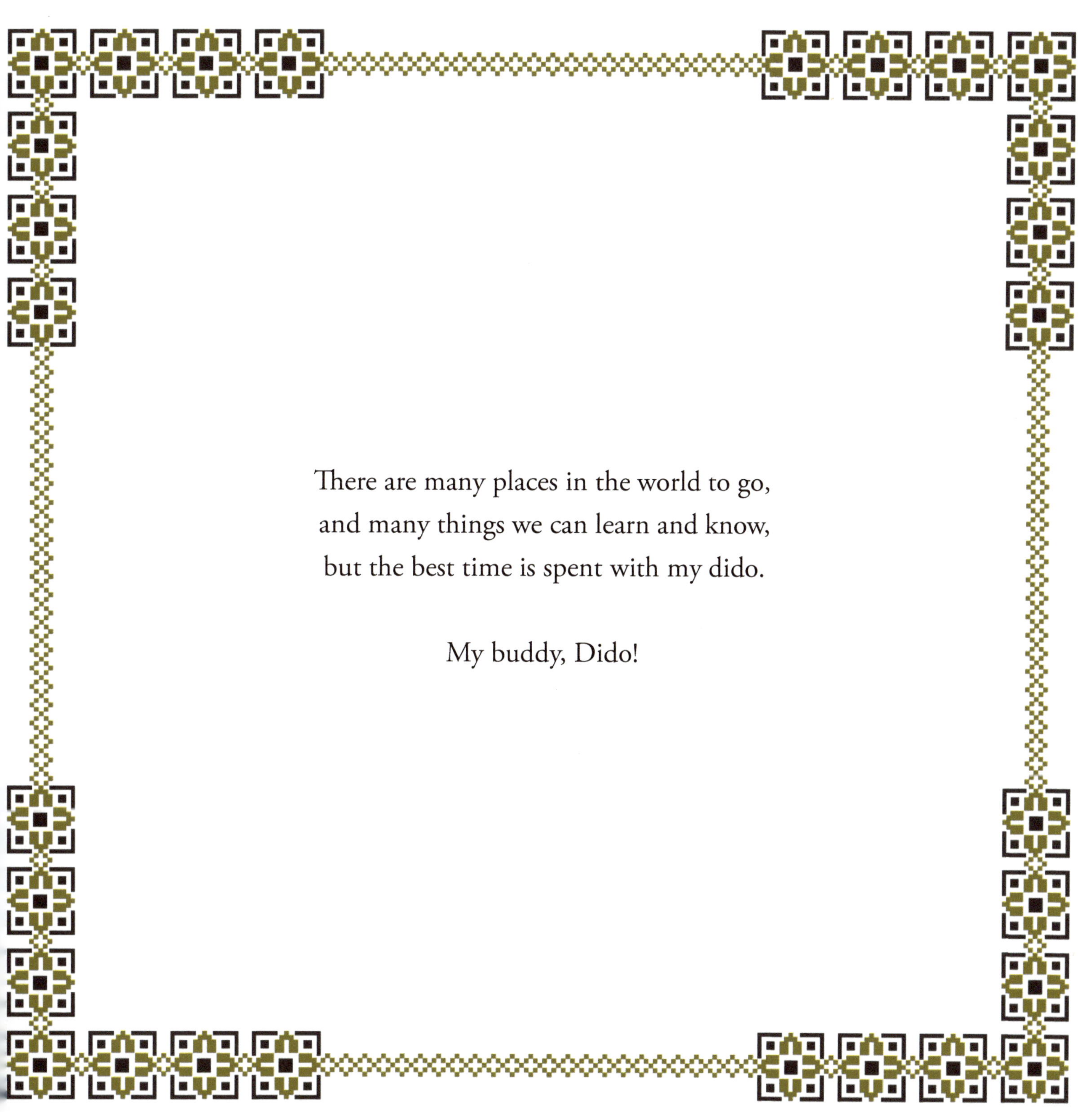

There are many places in the world to go,
and many things we can learn and know,
but the best time is spent with my dido.

My buddy, Dido!

So no more screens or computers galore.
Give me my dido to play on the floor.
His jokes and stories mean so much more.

My buddy, Dido!

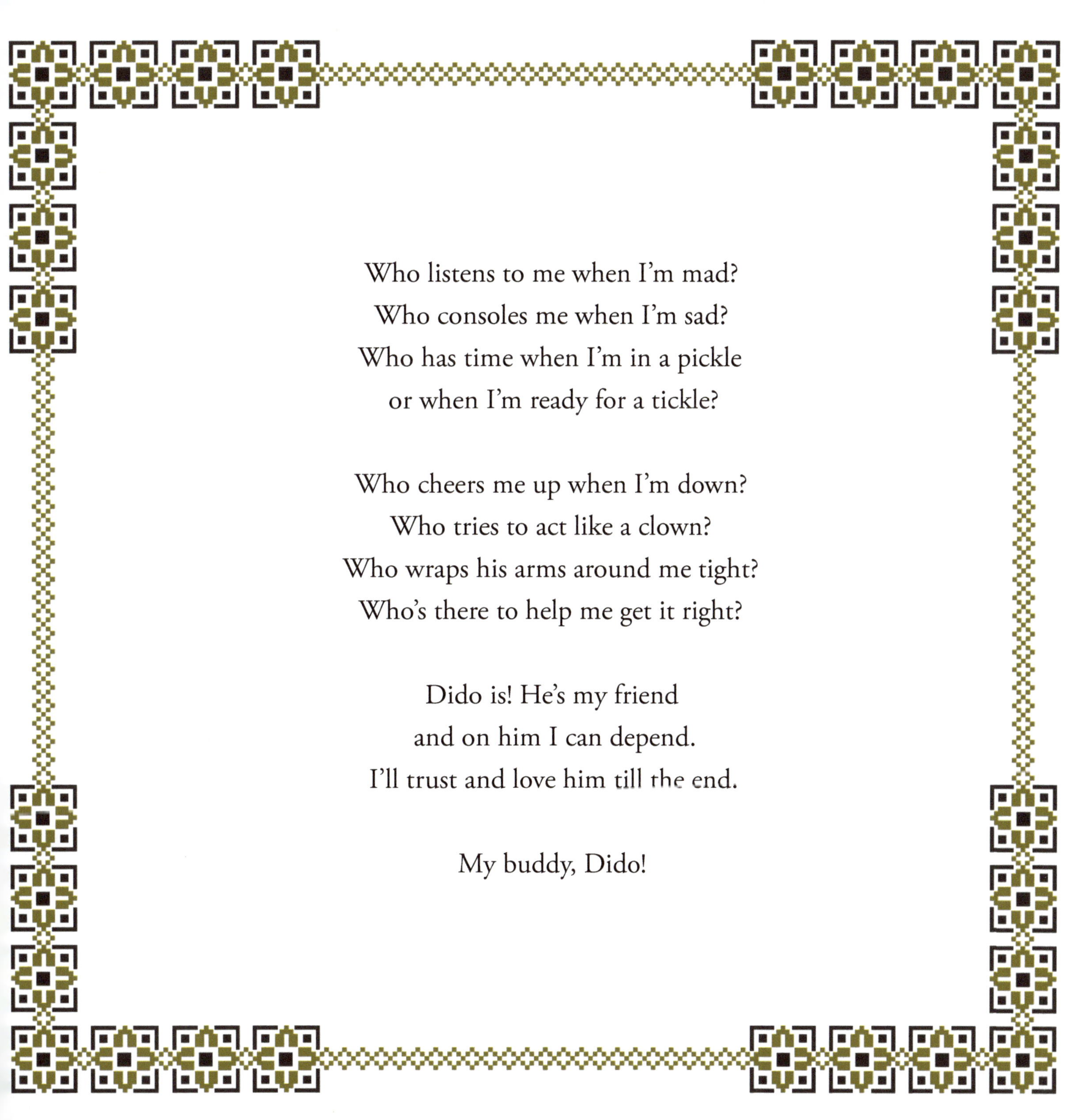

Who listens to me when I'm mad?
Who consoles me when I'm sad?
Who has time when I'm in a pickle
or when I'm ready for a tickle?

Who cheers me up when I'm down?
Who tries to act like a clown?
Who wraps his arms around me tight?
Who's there to help me get it right?

Dido is! He's my friend
and on him I can depend.
I'll trust and love him till the end.

My buddy, Dido!

So it's important, you know it's true,
to call our didos and say thank you.
And tell them that we love them, too!

My buddy, Dido!

Giant, short, plump or small.
Thin-haired, long-haired, toupée-haired, bald.
Every colour, build and size.
Cheerful, silly, fun-loving, wise.

My buddy, Dido!

Dido August's Holushki Soup Recipe

Soup:

3 tablespoons butter
1 large onion, chopped
2 cups beef or chicken broth
Boiling water to fill medium-sized pot
½ cup carrots, sliced
½ cup peas, shelled
Salt and pepper to taste

Noodles:

2 cups flour
2 eggs
1 tsp salt
Enough water to mix dough until firm

Sauté the onions in butter in a medium-sized pot, add beef or chicken broth, and continue to sauté. Then add boiling water to pot until it is ¾ full. Add carrots and peas. Add the dough mixture by teaspoonful one at a time to boiling broth. Add salt and pepper to taste. Simmer soup until the dough noodles have cooked. Noodles are done when they rise to the top and are tender but firm. When the carrots, peas and dough noodles are cooked, remove from heat. Serve with homemade bread. Enjoy!

Marion Mutala

Marion Mutala has a master's degree in educational administration and taught for 30 years. With a passion for the arts, she loves to write, sing, play pickleball and guitar, travel and read. Marion has written nineteen books to date, many of which have won or been shortlisted for various awards. She is the author of the National Bestselling, Award-winning children's book series *Baba's Babushka*, including a limited edition hardcover of *Baba's Babushka: Magical Ukrainian Adventures*. Marion recently published her second book of poetry, *Race to Finish*, in 2021 and her first cookbook, *Baba Sophie's Ukrainian Cookbook*, in 2022. *Baba's Over the Moon*, dedicated to her first grandchild and her nineteenth book, was released recently.

www.babasbabushka.ca

Olha Tkachenko

Artist and illustrator Olha Tkachenko was born in Ukraine, a country of rich art traditions. Having grown up in a family of artists, she began drawing and painting at a very young age. She received formal education at a fine arts school and has worked in the visual arts all her life, showing her works at art events in Canada, Ukraine, and France. In 2014, Olha moved with her family to Canada and enjoys the opportunity to continue her art in this beautiful country; the Ukrainian-Canadian community, and its focus on national heritage, has inspired new art projects.